A KNITTED SOCK SOCIETY

10 SOCK DESIGNS USING ROWAN FINE ART

BY RACHEL COOPEY

QUAIL

A KNITTED SOCK SOCIETY

10 SOCK DESIGNS USING ROWAN FINE ART

BY RACHEL COOPEY

Technical Editor: Sarah Hatton

Photography by Sam Sloan

QUAIL

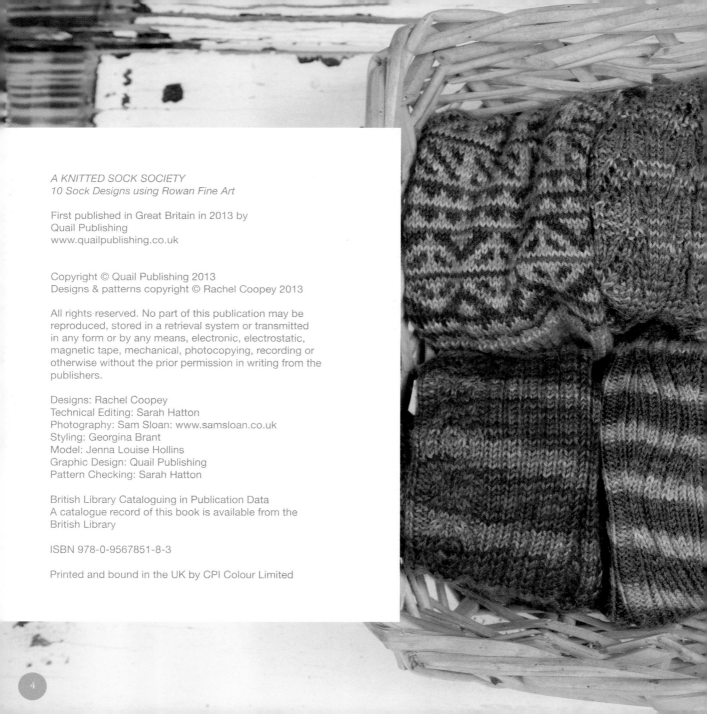

A KNITTED SOCK SOCIETY
10 Sock Designs using Rowan Fine Art

First published in Great Britain in 2013 by
Quail Publishing
www.quailpublishing.co.uk

Designs: Rachel Coopey
Technical Editing: Sarah Hatton
Photography: Sam Sloan: www.samsloan.co.uk
Styling: Georgina Brant
Model: Jenna Louise Hollins
Graphic Design: Quail Publishing
Pattern Checking: Sarah Hatton

British Library Cataloguing in Publication Data
A catalogue record of this book is available from the
British Library

ISBN 978-0-9567851-8-3

Printed and bound in the UK by CPI Colour Limited

ENID *pg. 32*

CONTENTS

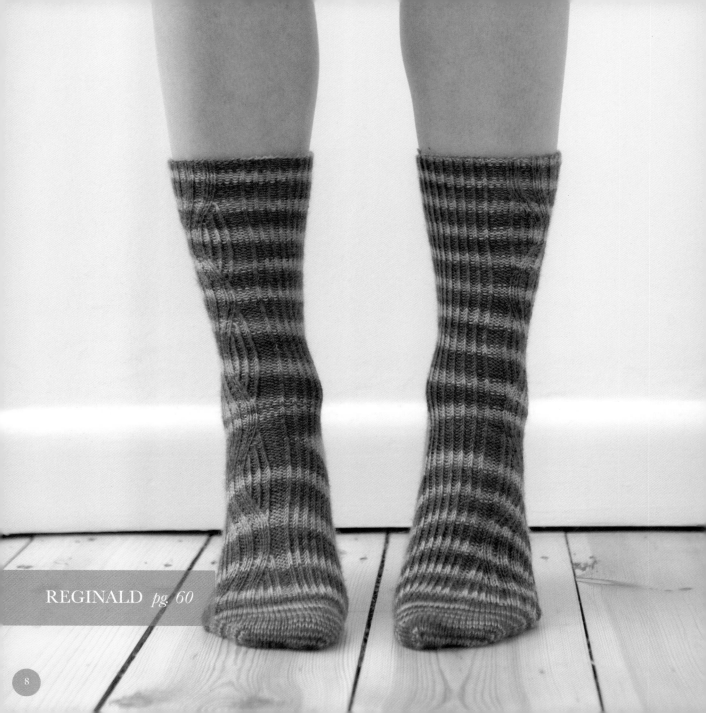

REGINALD *pg 60*

INTRODUCTION

I was taught to knit by my grandmother and mother and I've still got the extremely long garter stitch stitch scarf to prove it! I was drawn to sock knitting by sock yarn, I bought 3 skeins of hand-dyed sock yarn because they were so beautiful and thought I'd give knitting a pair of socks a try. When I turned the heel on that first sock I felt like I'd performed a magic trick, I pulled it out of my knitting bag and showed it to everyone I came across, shouting 'Look, look what I made! It's a SOCK!' (I got varying degrees of enthusiasm in return, but I think it's fair to say no-one was as excited as me). I haven't stopped knitting and designing socks since then, I love the portability of socks, the intricacy and the usefulness of the finished project - there's nothing like hand knitted socks for keeping your feet warm.

Rachel x

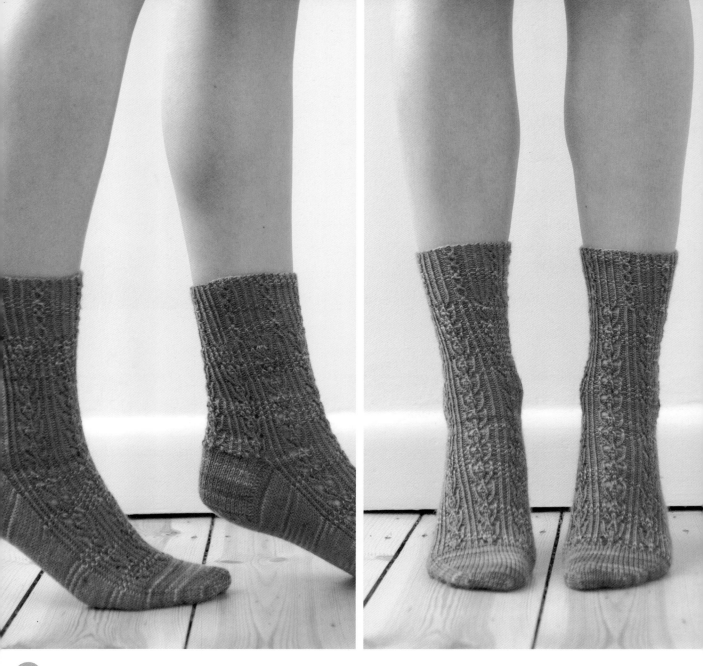

ENID

Page 32

Rowan Fine Art
SH 302
Tawny

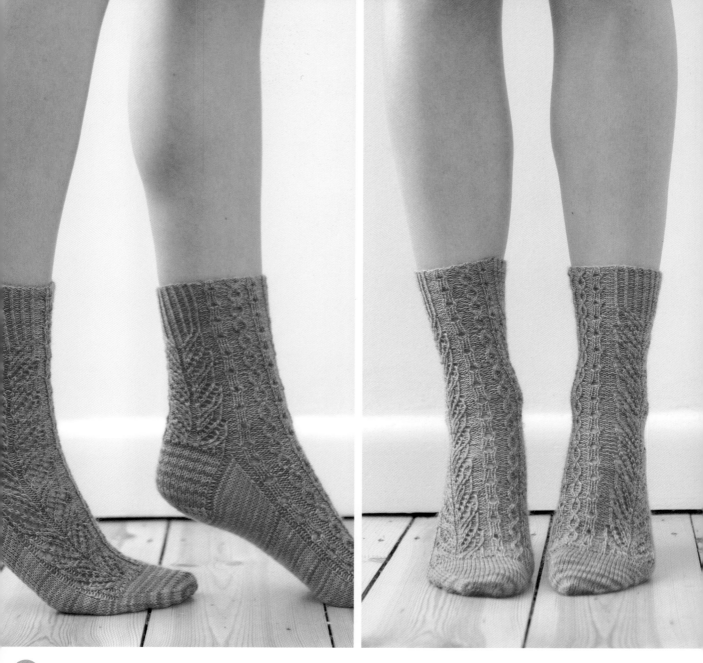

HEBE

Page 36

Rowan Fine Art
SH 301
Serin

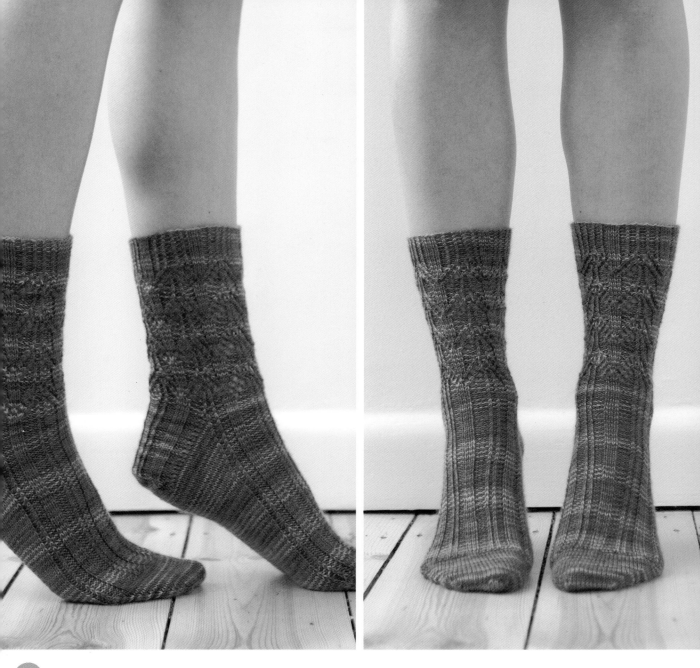

HECTOR

Page 40

Rowan Fine Art
SH 307
Pheasant

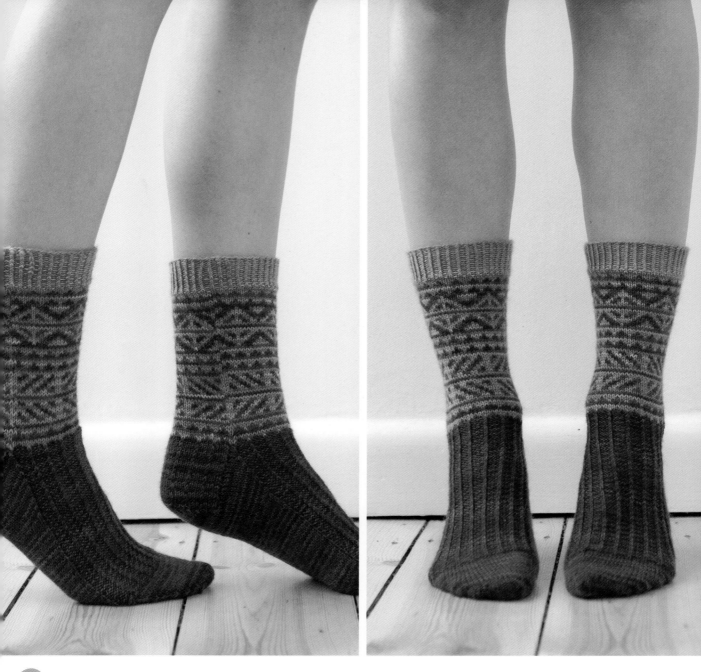

JESSE

Page 44

Rowan Fine Art
SH 303 Waxwing
SH 301 Serin

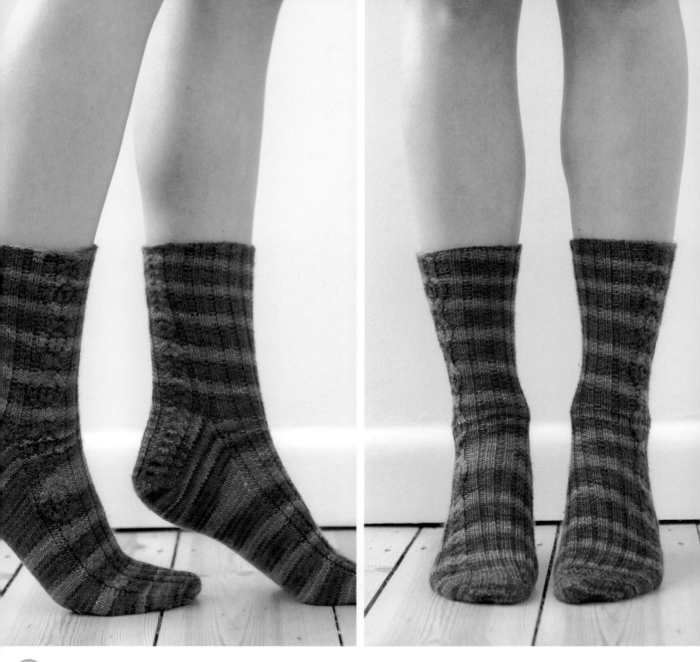

LAURIE

Page 48

Rowan Fine Art
SH 305
Kingfisher

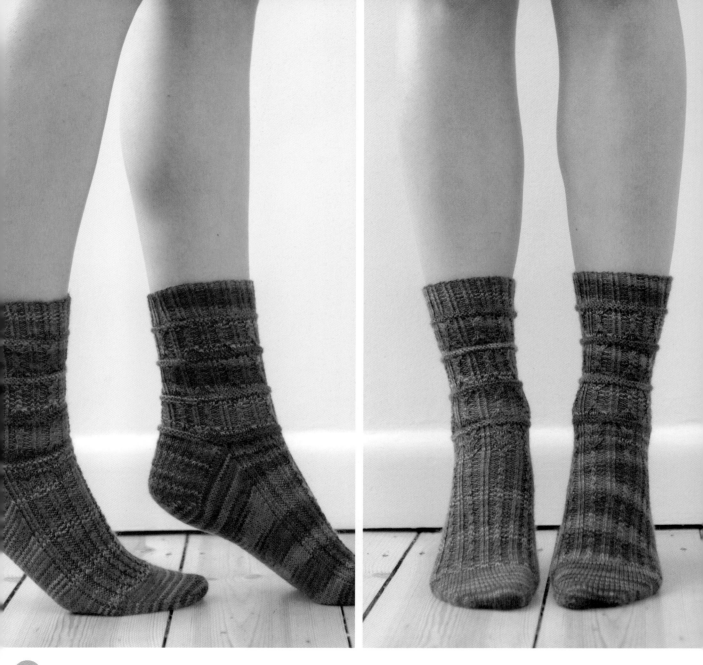

MAGNUS

Page 52

Rowan Fine Art
SH 305 Kingfisher
SH 306 Lapwing

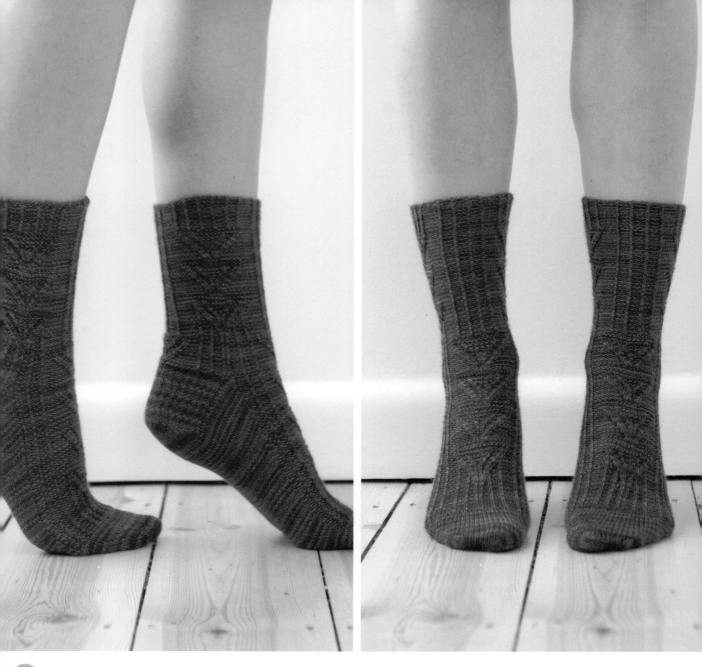

OGDEN

Page 56

Rowan Fine Art
SH 303
Waxwing

REGINALD

Page 60

Rowan Fine Art
SH 308
Chiff-Chaff

THORA

Page 64

Rowan Fine Art
SH 304
Raven

ELLERY

Page 70

Rowan Fine Art
SH 306
Lapwing

THE PATTERNS

ENID

Sizes - Foot circumference

S	M	L	
20	23	25	cm
8	9	10	in

YARN
Rowan Fine Art
For all sizes
1 skein of shade 302 – Tawny

NEEDLES
2.5mm (UK 13) (US 1½) 80cm/32in circular needles or
DPNs or size needed to achieve tension.
Cable Needle
Tapestry Needle

TENSION
36 sts and 50 rows to 10cm/4in measured over st st
using 2.5mm (US 1½) needles.

PATTERN NOTE
Please note there are different instructions for the left
and right socks.
Increase 1 to 3: Knit, purl, knit in to the next stitch,
2 stitches increased.
Wrap 3: K1tbl, p1, k1tbl onto cable needle, wrap yarn
twice around these stitches by bringing yarn to front
of work between the left needle and the cable needle
and wrapping yarn to back of work between cable
needle and right needle, then slip the 3 stitches from
the cable needle to the right needle.

Cuff
Cast on 60 [70:80] sts.
Join to work in the round, being careful not to twist.
Work the 6 rounds of Cuff chart 5 times.

Leg
Work the 8 rounds of leg chart 6 times, then work
rounds 1 to 3 once more.

For Small and Large only: P1, k1tbl.

For all sizes
Heel Flap
Turn work so **WS** is facing.
Heel Flap will now be worked back and forth on the
next 29[35:39] sts, beg with a **WS** row.
Keep rem 31 [35:41] sts on needles for instep.

Row 1 (WS): Sl1 pwise wyif, p28 [34:38].
Row 2 (RS): *Sl1 pwise wyib, k1, rep from * until 1 st
rem, k1.

Work these 2 rows 15 times then work row 1 once
more.

Turn Heel
Row 1 (RS): Sl1 wyib, k15 [19:21], ssk, k1, turn.
Row 2: Sl1 wyif, p4 [6:6], p2tog, p1, turn.
Row 3: Sl1 wyib, k to 1 st before gap, ssk, k1, turn.
Row 4: Sl1 wyif, p to 1 st before gap, p2tog, p1, turn.
Rep rows 3 and 4 until all sts have been worked.
17 [21:23] heel sts rem.

Gusset
Set-up Round: Sl 1, k16 [20:22], pick up and knit 16 sts
along edge of heel flap (1 st in each
slipped st, work round 1 of instep chart repeat sts
within red border 3(3,4) times before completing the
chart, pick up and knit 16 sts along
edge of heel flap. 80 [88:96] sts.
K33 [37:39]. The start of the round is now at start of
instep stitches.
Round 1: Work in pattern across instep sts, ssk, k to
last 2 sts of round, k2tog.

Round 2: Work in pattern across instep sts, knit to end. Rep these 2 rounds 8 [8:6] more times. 62 [70:82] sts rem, 31 [35:41] sts each on instep and sole.

Foot
Cont working evenly in patt as set until the sock measures 5cm/2in less than the desired foot length.

Toe
Round 1: Knit.
Round 2: K1, ssk, knit to 3 sts before end of instep, k2tog, k2, ssk, knit until 3 sts remain, k2tog, k1.

Rep these 2 rounds until 20 [24:24] sts rem.
Cut yarn, leaving a 30cm/12in tail.
Graft sts together using Kitchener stitch. Weave in ends.

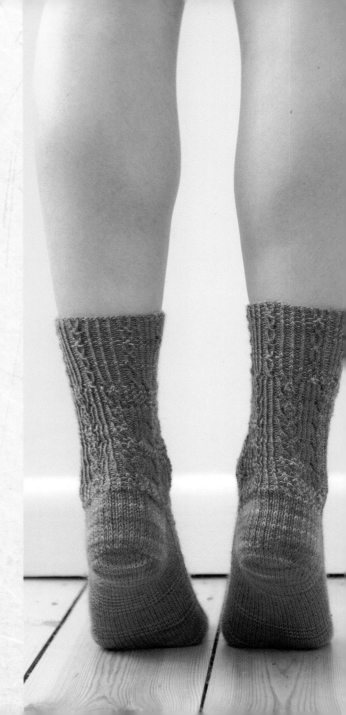

CHARTS

Instep Medium

Cuff Chart

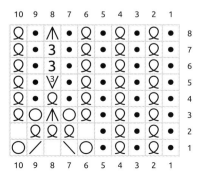

Leg Chart

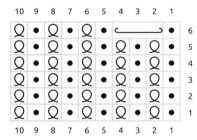

Instep Small & Large

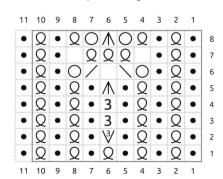

Key

☐	knit
ℚ	ktbl
○	yo
╱	k2tog
╲	ssk
⋀	cdd
V₃	increase 1 to 3
3	knit 3
•	purl
⌐___⌐	wrap 3
☐	repeat

HEBE

Sizes - Foot circumference

S	L	
20-23	23-25	cm
8-9	9-10	in

YARN
Rowan Fine Art
For all sizes
1 skein of shade 301 – Serin

NEEDLES
2.5mm (UK 13) (US 1½) 80cm/32in circular needles or DPNs or size needed to achieve tension.
Cable Needle
Tapestry Needle

TENSION
36 sts and 50 rows to 10cm/4in measured over st st using 2.5mm (US 1½) needles.

1/1 LPC: Slip next st to cable needle and place at front of work, p1, then k1 from cable needle.
1/1 RPC: Slip next st to cable needle and place at back of work, k1, then p1 from cable needle.
1/1 LPT: Slip next st to cable needle and place at front of work, p1, then k1 tbl from cable needle.
1/1 RPT: Slip next st to cable needle and place at back of work, k1 tbl, then p1 from cable needle.
1/1 RT: Slip next st to cable needle and place at back of work, k1 tbl, then k1 tbl from cable needle.
1/1 LT: Slip next st to cable needle and place at front of work, k1 tbl, then k1 tbl from cable needle.

Cuff
Cast on 66 [76] sts.
Join to work in the round, being careful not to twist.

Left Sock: *Work round 1 of Chart A[D], work round 1 of Chart B, rep from * once more.

Right Sock: * Work round 1 of Chart B, work round 1 of Chart A[E], rep from * once more.

For both socks
Working in pattern as set, repeat rounds 1-8 of the Charts three times before working rounds 9-16 once. (32 rounds)

Leg

Left Sock: *Work round 1 of Chart A[D], work round 1 of Chart C, rep from * once more.

Right Sock: * Work round 1 of Chart C, work round 1 of Chart A[E], rep from * once more.

For both socks
Cont in pattern as set until Charts have been completed three times. (48 rounds)

Heel Flap
Turn work so **WS** is facing.
Heel Flap will now be worked back and forth on the next 33[38] sts, beg with a **WS** row.
Keep rem 33 [38] sts on needles for instep.

Row 1 (WS): Sl1 pwise wyif, p32 [37].
Row 2 (RS): *Sl1 pwise wyib, k1, rep from * until 1 st rem, k1.

Work these 2 rows 15 times then work row 1 once more.

Turn Heel
Row 1 (RS): Sl1 wyib, k17 [20], ssk, k1, turn.
Row 2: Sl1 wyif, p4 [5], p2tog, p1, turn.
Row 3: Sl1 wyib, k to 1 st before gap, ssk, k1, turn.
Row 4: Sl1 wyif, p to 1 st before gap, p2tog, p1, turn.
Rep rows 3 and 4 until all sts have been worked.
19 [22] heel sts rem.

Gusset

Set-up Round: Sl 1, k18 [21], pick up and knit 16 sts along edge of heel flap (1 st in each slipped st).

Left Sock: Work round 1 of Chart A[D], work round 1 of Chart C.

Right Sock: Work round 1 of Chart C, work round 1 of Chart A[E].

For both socks

Pick up and knit 16 sts along edge of heel flap, 84 [92] sts.
K38 [40]. The start of the round is now at start of instep stitches.

Round 1: Work in pattern across instep sts, ssk, k to last 2 sts of round, k2tog.
Round 2: Work in pattern across instep sts, knit to end.
Rep these 2 rounds 8 [7] more times. 66 [76] sts rem, 33 [38] on instep and 33[38] on sole.

Foot

Cont working evenly in patt as set until the sock measures 5cm/2in less than the desired foot length.

Toe

Round 1: Knit.
Round 2: K1, ssk, knit to 3 sts before end of instep, k2tog, k2, ssk, knit until 3 sts remain, k2tog, k1.

Rep these 2 rounds until 18 [24] sts rem.
Cut yarn, leaving a 30cm/12in tail.
Graft sts together using Kitchener stitch. Weave in ends.

CHARTS

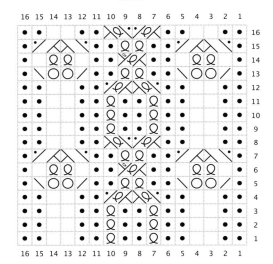

Chart A

Chart B

Chart C

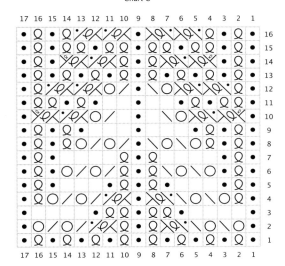

Chart D – Left

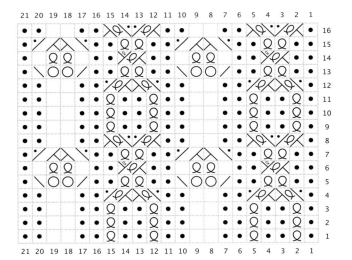

Chart E – Right

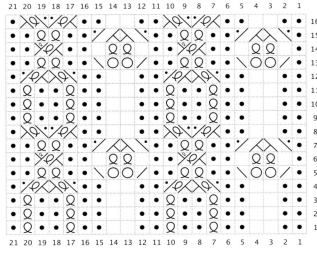

Key

☐	knit
Ω	ktbl
○	yo
╱	k2tog
╲	ssk
Λ	cdd
₩	increase 1 to 3
3	knit 3
•	purl
⌣	wrap 3

HECTOR

Sizes - Foot circumference

S	M	L	
20	23	25	cm
8	9	10	in

YARN
Rowan Fine Art
For all sizes
1 skein of shade 307 Pheasant

NEEDLES
2.5mm (UK 13) (US 1½) 80cm/32in circular needles or DPNs or size needed to achieve tension.
Tapestry Needle

TENSION
36 sts and 50 rows to 10cm/4in measured over st st using 2.5mm (US 1½) needles.

Cuff
Cast on 60 [72:84] sts.
Join to work in the round, being careful not to twist.

Work round 1 of the cuff chart 16 times, then continue to work the remainder of the Cuff chart.

Leg
Work the Leg chart 3 times and then work rounds 1- 4 once more.

Heel Set-up
For Small & Large only: P1, k1tbl, p1.

For all sizes
Heel Flap
Turn work so **WS** is facing.
Heel Flap will now be worked back and forth on the next 29[35:41] sts, beg with a **WS** row.

Keep rem 31 [37:43] sts on needles for instep.

For Small & Large only
Row 1 (WS): Sl1 pwise wyif, (p1tbl, k1 p1tbl, k3, p3, k3) 2 [-:3] times, p1tbl, k1, p1tbl, p1.
Row 2 (RS): *Sl1 pwise wyib, (k1tbl, p1, k1tbl, p3, k3, p3) 2 [-:3] times, k1tbl, p1, k1tbl, k1.

For Medium only
Row 1 (WS): Sl1 pwise wyif, (k3, p3, k3, p1tbl, k1, p1tbl) 2 times, k3, p3, k3, p1.
Row 2 (RS): *Sl1 pwise wyib, (p3, k3, p3, k1tbl, p1, k1tbl) 2 times, p3, k3, p3, k1.

For all sizes
Work these 2 rows 15 times then work row 1 once more.

Turn Heel
Row 1 (RS): Sl1 wyib, k15 [19:21], ssk, k1, turn.
Row 2: Sl1 wyif, p4 [6:4], p2tog, p1, turn.
Row 3: Sl1 wyib, k to 1 st before gap, ssk, k1, turn.
Row 4: Sl1 wyif, p to 1 st before gap, p2tog, p1, turn.
Rep rows 3 and 4 until all sts have been worked.
17 [21:23] heel sts rem.

Gusset
Set-up Round: Sl 1, k16 [20:22], pick up and knit 16 sts along edge of heel flap (1 st in each slipped st, work across 31 [37:43] instep sts as folls:-

Small: (P2, k3, p3, (k1tbl, p1) 2 times) 2 times, p2, k3, p2.
Medium: (p1, k1tbl, p3, k3, p3, k1tbl) 3 times, p1.
Large: (P2, k3, p3, (k1tbl, p1) 2 times) 3 times, p2, k3, p2.

For all sizes
Pick up and knit 16 sts along edge of heel flap.
80 [90:98] sts.
K33 [37:39]. The start of the round is now at start of instep stitches.

Round 1: Work in pattern across instep sts, ssk, k to

last 2 sts of round, k2tog.
Round 2: Work in pattern across instep sts, knit to end.
Rep these 2 rounds 9 [8:6] more times.
60 [72:84] sts rem, 31 [37:43] on instep and 29 [35:41] on sole.

Foot

Cont working evenly in patt as set until the sock measures 5cm/2in less than the desired foot length.

Toe

Set up round: K1, ssk, knit to 3 sts before end of instep, k2tog, k to end. 58 [70:82] sts rem, 29 [35:41] on instep and sole.

Round 1: Knit.
Round 2: K1, ssk, knit to 3 sts before end of instep, k2tog, k2, ssk, knit until 3 sts remain, k2tog, k1.

Rep these 2 rounds until 18 [22:22] sts rem.
Cut yarn, leaving a 30cm/12in tail.
Graft sts together using Kitchener stitch. Weave in ends.

CHARTS

Cuff

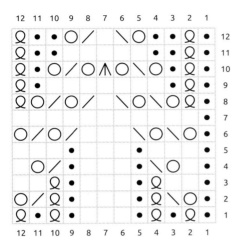

Leg

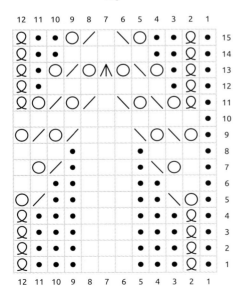

Key

☐	knit
Ϙ	ktbl
•	purl
◯	yo
╲	ssk
╱	k2tog
⋀	Cdd

JESSE

Sizes - Foot circumference

S	M	L	
20	23	25	cm
8	9	10	in

YARN
Rowan Fine Art
For all sizes
1 skein each of
A – shade 303 Waxwing
B – shade 301 Serin

NEEDLES
2.5mm (UK 13) (US 1½) 80cm/32in circular needles or
DPNs or size needed to achieve tension.
Tapestry Needle

TENSION
36 sts and 50 rows to 10cm/4in measured over st st
using 2.5mm (US 1½) needles.

PATTERN NOTE
Please note there are different charts for the left and
right socks.

Cuff
Using B, cast on 60 [72:84] sts.
Join to work in the round, being careful not to twist.
Rib Round: *K1 tbl, p1, rep from * to end.
Work this round 15 more times.

Leg
Working from correct chart, cont in patt as set until the
chart has been completed. Cut B leaving a 15cm/6in
tail, the rest of the sock will be worked with yarn A.

Heel Flap
Turn work so **WS** is facing.
Heel Flap will now be worked back and forth on the
next 29[37:41] sts, beg with a **WS** row and using A
throughout.
Keep rem 31 [35:43] sts on needles for instep.
Row 1 (WS): Sl wyif, p28 [36:40].

Row 2 (RS): * Sl wyib, k3, rep from * to last st of row,
k1.
Rep these 2 rows 14 times more, then work row 1 once
more, ending with RS facing for next row.

Turn Heel
Row 1 (RS): Sl1 wyib, k15 [19:21], ssk, k1, turn.
Row 2: Sl1 wyif, p4, p2tog, p1, turn.
Row 3: Sl1 wyib, k to 1 st before gap, ssk, k1, turn.
Row 4: Sl1 wyif, p to 1 st before gap, p2tog, p1, turn.
Rep rows 3 and 4 until all sts have been worked.
17 [21:23] heel sts rem.

Gusset
Set-up Round: Sl 1, k18 [20:24], pick up and knit 16 sts
along edge of heel flap (1 st in each
slipped st, work across instep sts as folls:- p3, (k1tbl,
p3) 7[8:10] times, pick up and knit 16 sts along edge of
heel flap. 80 [88:98] sts.
K33 [37:39]. The start of the round is now at start of
instep stitches, this round also sets pattern across
instep sts.

Round 1: Work in pattern as set across instep sts, ssk, k
to last 2 sts of round, k2tog.
Round 2: Work in pattern across instep sts, knit to end.
Rep these 2 rounds 10 [8:7] more times. 60 [70:84] sts
rem, 31 [35:43] on instep and 29 [35:41] on sole.

Foot
Cont working evenly in patt as set until the sock
measures 5cm/2in less than the desired foot length.

Small and Large only:
K1, ssk, k to 3 sts before end of instep, k2tog, k to end.
58 [70:82] sts rem, 29 [35:41] on instep and sole.

For all sizes:
Toe
Round 1: Knit.
Round 2: K1, ssk, k to 3 sts before end of instep, k2tog,
k2, ssk, knit until 3 sts rem, k2tog, k1.
Rep these 2 rounds until 18 [22:22] sts rem.
Cut yarn, leaving a 30cm/12in tail.
Graft sts together using Kitchener stitch. Weave in
ends.

CHARTS

Left Chart

12 11 10 9 8 7 6 5 4 3 2 1

57
56
55
54
53
52
51
50
49
48
47
46
45
44
43
42
41
40
39
38
37
36
35
34
33
32
31
30
29
28
27
26
25
24
23
22
21
20
19
18
17
16
15
14
13
12
11
10
9
8
7
6
5
4
3
2
1

12 11 10 9 8 7 6 5 4 3 2 1

Right Chart

12 11 10 9 8 7 6 5 4 3 2 1

57
56
55
54
53
52
51
50
49
48
47
46
45
44
43
42
41
40
39
38
37
36
35
34
33
32
31
30
29
28
27
26
25
24
23
22
21
20
19
18
17
16
15
14
13
12
11
10
9
8
7
6
5
4
3
2
1

12 11 10 9 8 7 6 5 4 3 2 1

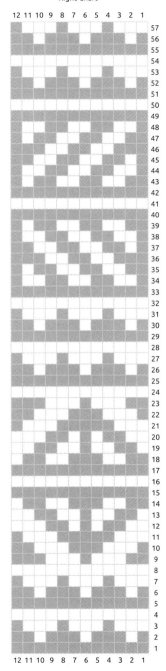

Key

☐ A

▨ B

LAURIE

Sizes - Foot circumference

S	M	L	
20	23	25	cm
8	9	10	in

YARN
Rowan Fine Art
For all sizes
1 skein of shade 305 Kingfisher

NEEDLES
2.5mm (UK 13) (US 1½) 80cm/32in circular needles or DPNs or size needed to achieve tension.
Cable Needle
Tapestry Needle

TENSION
36 sts and 50 rows to 10cm/4in measured over st st using 2.5mm (US 1½) needles.

2/2 RC: Slip next 2 sts to cable needle and place at back of work, k2, then k2 from cable needle.
2/2 LC: Slip next 2 sts to cable needle and place at front of work, k2, then k2 from cable needle.
2/1 RPC: Slip next st to cable needle and place at back of work, k2, then p1 from cable needle.
2/1 LPC: Slip next 2 sts to cable needle and place at front of work, p1, then k2 from cable needle.
1/1 RC: Slip next st to cable needle and place at back of work, k1, then k1 from cable needle.
1/1 LC: Slip next st to cable needle and place at front of work, k1, then k1 from cable needle.

Pattern note: Please note there are different instructions for the left and right socks.

Cuff
Using B, cast on 62 [70:78] sts.
Join to work in the round, being careful not to twist.

Left Sock only
*P2, k2, rep from * 4(5,6) times, p3, work row 1 of Chart A, p3, *k2, p2, rep from * 5(6,7) times, work row 1 of Chart A, p2, k2.

Right Sock only
P3, work row 1 of Chart A, p3, *k2, p2, rep from * 5(6,7) times, work row 1 of Chart A, *p2, k2, rep from * to 5(6,7) times.

For both socks
Continue to work in this way until Chart A has been completed 4 times.

Leg
Left Sock only
*P2, k2, rep from * 4(5,6) times, work row 1 of Chart B, *k2, p2, rep from * 5(6,7) times, work row 1 of Chart A, p2, k2.

Right Sock only
Work row 1 of Chart B, *k2, p2, rep from * 5(6,7) times, work row 1 of Chart A, *p2, k2, rep from * to 5(6,7) times.

For both socks
Continue to work in this way until Chart B has been completed 3 times.

Heel Flap
Turn work so **WS** is facing.
Heel Flap will now be worked back and forth on the next 32[36:40] sts, beg with a **WS** row.
Keep rem 30 [34:38] sts on needles for instep.
Left Sock only
Row 1 (WS): Sl1 pwise wyif, p1, k2, p8, *k2, p2, rep from * 5(6,7) times.
Row 2 (RS): Sl1 pwise wyib, k1, *p2, k2, rep from * 4(5,6) times. p2, k8, p2, k2.
Row 3 (WS): Sl1 pwise wyif, p1, k2, p8, *k2, p2, rep from * 5(6,7) times.
Row 4 (RS): Sl1 pwise wyib, k1, *p2, k2, rep from * 4(5,6) times. p2, 2/2 RC, 2/2 LC, p2, k2.
Right Sock only
Row 1 (WS): Sl1 pwise wyif, p1, *k2, p2, rep from * 4(5,6) times, k2, p8, k2, p2.
Row 2 (RS): Sl1 pwise wyib, k1, p2, k8, *p2, k2 rep from * 5(6,7) times.
Row 3 (WS): Sl1 pwise wyif, p1, *k2, p2, rep from *

4(5,6) times, k2, p8, k2, p2.
Row 4 (RS): Sl1 pwise wyib, k1, p2, 2/2 RC, 2/2 LC , *p2, k2 rep from * 5(6,7) times.

For both socks
Work these 4 rows 7 times then work rows 1-3 once more.

Turn Heel
Row 1 (RS): Sl1 wyib, k18 [20:22], ssk, k1, turn.
Row 2: Sl1 wyif, p7, p2tog, p1, turn.
Row 3: Sl1 wyib, k to 1 st before gap, ssk, k1, turn.
Row 4: Sl1 wyif, p to 1 st before gap, p2tog, p1, turn.
Rep rows 3 and 4 until all sts have been worked.
20 [22:24] heel sts rem.

Gusset
Set-up Round: Sl 1, k19 [21:23], pick up and knit 16 sts along edge of heel flap (1 st in each
slipped st, work Instep Pattern across 30 [34:38] sts;
Instep Pattern:
Left Sock:*P2, k2, rep from * 4(5,6) times, work row 1 of Chart B.
Right Sock: Work row 1 of Chart B, *k2, p2, rep from * 4(5,6) times.
For both socks: Pick up and knit 16 sts along edge of heel flap. 82 [88:94] sts.
K36 [38:40].

The start of the round is at start of instep stitches.
Round 1: Work in pattern across instep sts, ssk, k to last 2 sts of round, k2tog.
Round 2: Work in pattern across instep sts, knit to end.
Rep these 2 rounds 10 [9:8] times more. 60 [68:76] sts rem, 30 [34:38] each on instep and sole.

Foot
Cont working evenly in patt as set until Chart B has been completed 5 times in total.

Left Sock:*P2, k2, rep from * 4(5,6) times, p3, work row 1 Chart A, p3
Right Sock: P3, work row 1 of Chart A, p3, *k2, p2, rep from * 4(5,6) times.

Cont working evenly in patt as set until the sock measures 5cm/2in less than the desired foot length.

Toe
Round 1: K1, ssk, work in pattern (k the k sts, p the p sts) to 3 sts before end of instep, k2tog, k2, ssk, knit until 3 sts remain, k2tog, k1.
Round 2: Work sts in pattern.

Rep these 2 rounds until 20 [24:24] sts rem.
Cut yarn, leaving a 30cm/12in tail.
Graft sts together using Kitchener stitch. Weave in ends.

CHARTS

Chart A

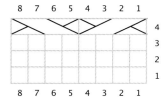

Chart B

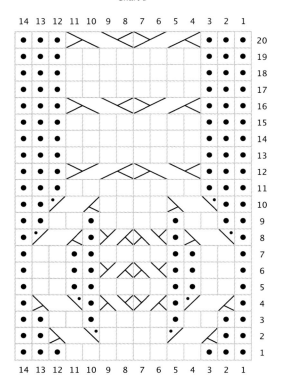

☐	knit
●	purl
	2/2 RC
	2/2 LC
	2/1 RPC
	2/1 LPC
	1/1 RC
	1/1 LC

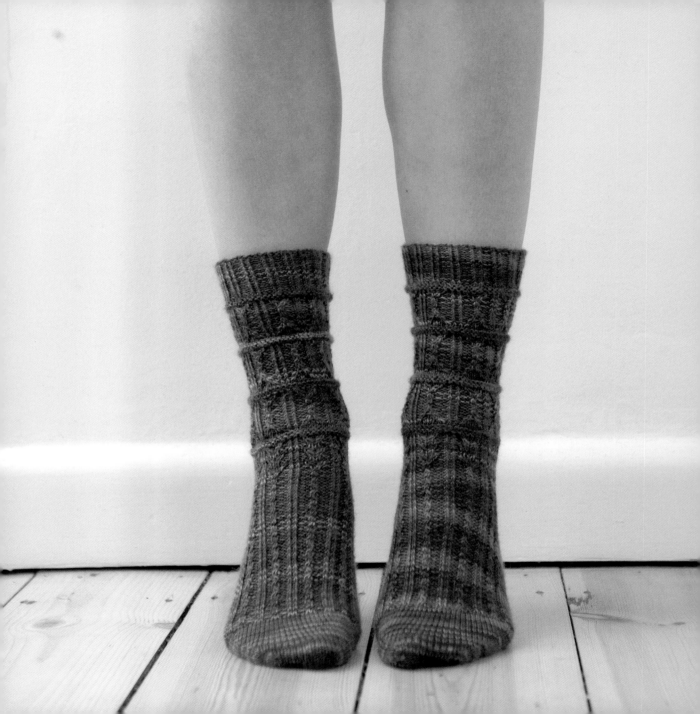

MAGNUS

Sizes - Foot circumference

S	M	L	
20	23	25	cm
8	9	10	in

YARN
Rowan Fine Art
For all sizes
1 skein each of
shade 305 Kingfisher
shade 306 Lapwing

NEEDLES
2.5mm (UK 13) (US 1½) 80cm/32in circular needles or
DPNs or size needed to achieve tension.
Cable Needle
Tapestry Needle

TENSION
36 sts and 50 rows to 10cm/4in measured over st st
using 2.5mm (US1½) needles.

PATTERN NOTES
Left Sock: Colour A is 305, colour B is 306.
Right Sock: Colour A is 306, colour B is 305.
You can make two identical socks if you prefer.

1/1 RPC: Slip next st to cable needle and place at back
of work, k1, then p1 from cable needle.
1/1 LPC: Slip next st to cable needle and place at front
of work, p1, then k1 from cable needle.
1/1 RC: Slip next st to cable needle and place at back
of work, k1, then k1 from cable needle.
1/1 LC: Slip next st to cable needle and place at front
of work, k1, then k1 from cable needle.

Cuff
Using A cast on 64 [72:80] sts.

Join to work in the round, being careful not to twist.
Rib Round: *K2 tbl, p2, rep from * to end.
Work this round 15 more times.
Leg
Using B work 19 rounds as set on leg chart.
Using A work 19 rounds as set on leg chart.
Using B work 19 rounds as set on leg chart.
Using A work from the leg chart until the rounds 1-4
have been completed.

Small & Large: K7.
Medium: K5.

Heel Flap
Turn work so **WS** is facing.
Heel Flap will now be worked back and forth on the
next 32[36:40] sts, beg with a **WS** row.
Keep rem 32 [36:40] sts on needles for instep.

Row 1 (WS): Sl1 wyif, p31 [35:39].
Row 2 (RS): *Sl1 wyib, k1, rep from * to last st of row,
k1.
Work these 2 rows 14 more times then work row 1
once more.
Turn Heel
Row 1 (RS): Sl1 wyib, k18 [20:22], ssk, k1, turn.
Row 2: Sl1 wyif, p7, p2tog, p1, turn.
Row 3: Sl1 wyib, k to 1 st before gap, ssk, k1, turn.
Row 4: Sl1 wyif, p to 1 st before gap, p2tog, p1, turn.
Rep rows 3 and 4 until all sts have been worked.
20 [22:24] heel sts rem.

Gusset
Set-up Round: Sl 1, k19 [21:23], pick up and knit 16 sts
along edge of heel flap (1 st in each
slipped st, work instep chart A across instep stitches
repeating the stitches within the red border 3 [4:4]
times, pick up and knit 16 sts along edge of heel flap.
84 [90:96] sts.
K36 [38:40]. The start of the round is now at start of
instep stitches.

Round 1: Work in pattern across instep sts, ssk, k to
last 2 sts of round, k2tog.

Round 2: Work in pattern across instep sts, knit to end.

Rep these 2 rounds 4 more times then work round 1 once more, Instep chart 1 has been completed 3 times. 72 [78:84] sts.

Round 1: Work instep chart B across instep stitches repeating the sts within the red border 3 [4:4] times, knit to end.
Round 2: Work in pattern across instep sts, ssk, k to last 2 sts of round, k2tog.
Rep these 2 rounds 3 [2:1] more times.
64 [72:80] sts rem, 32 [36:40] each on instep and sole.

Foot
Cont working evenly in patt as set until the sock meas 5cm/2in less than the desired foot length.

Toe
Round 1: K1, ssk, knit to 3 sts before end of instep, k2tog, k2, ssk, knit until 3 sts rem, k2tog, k1.
Round 2: Knit.

Rep these 2 rounds until 20 [24:24] sts rem.
Cut yarn, leaving a 30cm/12in tail.
Graft sts together using Kitchener stitch. Weave in ends.

CHARTS

Leg Chart

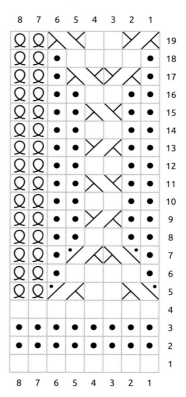

Instep Chart A Medium

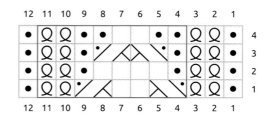

Instep Chart A Small & Large

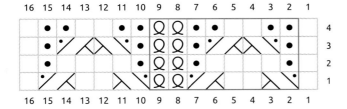

Instep Chart B Medium

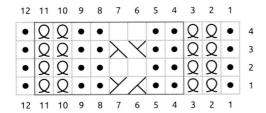

Instep Chart B Small & Large

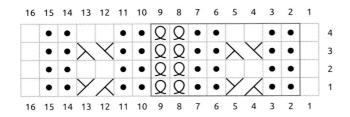

Key

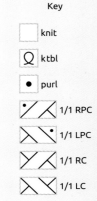

knit

ktbl

purl

1/1 RPC

1/1 LPC

1/1 RC

1/1 LC

repeat

OGDEN

Sizes - Foot circumference

S	L	
20-23	23-25	cm
8-9	9-10	in

YARN
Rowan Fine Art
For both sizes
1 skein of shade 303 – Waxwing

NEEDLES
2.5mm (UK 13) (US 1½) 80cm/32in circular needles or
DPNs or size needed to achieve tension.
Cable Needle
Tapestry Needle

TENSION
36 sts and 50 rows to 10cm/4in measured over st st
using 2.5mm (US 1½) needles.

1/1 LPT: Slip next st to cable needle and place at front
of work, p1, then k1 tbl from cable needle.
1/1 RPT: Slip next st to cable needle and place at back
of work, k1 tbl, then p1 from cable needle.
2/1 LPT: Slip next 2 sts to cable needle and place at
front of work, p1, then knit 2 stitches tbl from cable
needle.
2/1 RPT: Slip next st to cable needle and place at back
of work, knit 2 stitches tbl, then p1 from cable needle.
2/1 LT: Slip next 2 sts to cable needle and place at
front of work, k1, then k2 from cable needle.
2/1 RT: Slip next st to cable needle and place at back of
work, k2, then k1 from cable needle.

Cuff
Cast on 68 [76] sts.
Join to work in the round, being careful not to twist.

Rib round: *(K1tbl, p2) 5 times, k1tbl, p4 [6], (k1tbl, p2)
3 times, k1tbl, p4[6], rep from * once more.

Work the rib round 16 times.

Leg

*Work Chart A, p4[6], (k1tbl, p2) 3 times, k1tbl, p4[6],
rep from * once more.

Continue in pattern as set until Chart A has been
completed twice.

Next round: *Work Chart B, p4[6], (k1tbl, p2) 3 times,
k1tbl, p4[6], rep from * once more.

Continue in pattern as set until Chart B has been
completed once.

Next round: *P1, (k1tbl, p2) twice, k2tbl, (p2, k1tbl)
twice, p2[4], work Chart A, p1[3], rep from * once
more.

Continue in pattern as set until Chart A has been
completed once.

Heel Flap
Heel Set-up: P1, (k1tbl, p2) twice, k2tbl.
Turn work so **WS** is facing.
Heel Flap will now be worked back and forth on the
next 36[40] sts, beg with a **WS** row.
Keep rem 32 [36] sts on needles for instep.

Row 1 (WS): Sl1 pwise wyif, p35 [39].
Row 2 (RS): *Sl1 pwise wyib, k1, rep from * until 1 st
rem, k1.

Work these 2 rows 15 times then work row 1 once
more.

Turn Heel
Row 1 (RS): Sl1 wyib, k20 [22], ssk, k1, turn.
Row 2: Sl1 wyif, p7, p2tog, p1, turn.
Row 3: Sl1 wyib, k to 1 st before gap, ssk, k1, turn.

Row 4: Sl1 wyif, p to 1 st before gap, p2tog, p1, turn.
Rep rows 3 and 4 until all sts have been worked.
22 [24] heel sts rem.

Gusset

Set-up Round: Sl 1, k21 [23], pick up and knit 16 sts along edge of heel flap (1 st in each
slipped st, (p2, k1tbl) twice, p2[4], work Chart A, p2[4], (k1tbl, p2) twice , pick up and knit 16 sts along edge of heel flap. 86 [92] sts.
K38 [40]. The start of the round is now at start of instep stitches.

Round 1: Work in pattern across instep sts, ssk, k to last 2 sts of round, k2tog.
Round 2: Work in pattern across instep sts, knit to end.
Rep these 2 rounds 8 [6] more times. 66 [74] sts rem, 32 [36] on instep and 34[38] on sole.

Foot

Cont working evenly in patt as set until Chart A has been completed twice from the beginning of the gusset.

Next round: (P2, k1tbl) twice, p2[4], work Chart B, p2[4], (k1tbl, p2) twice, knit to end.

Continue in pattern as set until Chart B has been completed once.

(P2, k1tbl) twice, p3[5], (k1tbl, p2) twice, k2tbl, (p2, k1tbl) twice, p3[5], (k1tbl, p2) twice, knit to end.

Rep this round until the sock measures 5cm/2in less than the desired foot length.

Toe

Toe Set-up: K33[37], ssk, knit until 3 sts rem, k2tog, k1. 64 [72] sts rem, 32 [36] on instep and sole.
Round 1: Knit.
Round 2: K1, ssk, knit to 3 sts before end of instep, k2tog, k2, ssk, knit until 3 sts rem, k2tog, k1.

Rep these 2 rounds until 20 [24] sts rem.
Cut yarn, leaving a 30cm/12in tail.

Graft sts together using Kitchener stitch. Weave in ends.

CHARTS

Chart A

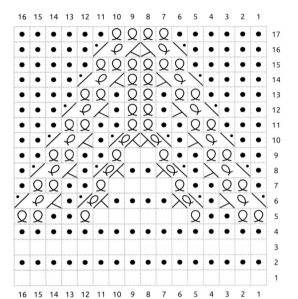

Key

☐	knit
●	purl
Ȣ	ktbl
⤬Ȣ⟍	1/1 LPT
⟋Ȣ⤬	1/1 RPT
⟍Ȣ˙	2/1 LPT
˙Ȣ⟍	2/1 RPT
⟍Ȣ⤬	2/1 LT
⤬Ȣ⟍	2/1 RT

Chart B

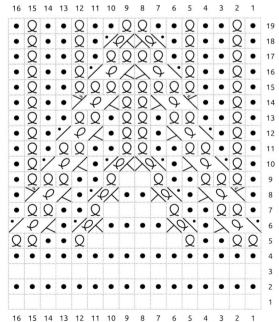

REGINALD

Sizes - Foot circumference

S	M	L	
20	23	25	cm
8	9	10	in

Small - Foot circumference 8 inches (Medium - 9 inches, Large - 10 inches)

YARN
Rowan Fine Art
For all sizes
1 skein of shade 308 Chiff-Chaff

NEEDLES
2.5mm (UK 13) (US 1½) 80cm/32in circular needles or DPNs or size needed to achieve tension.
Tapestry Needle

TENSION
36 sts and 50 rows to 10cm/4in measured over st st using 2.5mm (US 1½) needles.

PATTERN NOTE
Please note there are different instructions for the left and right socks.

Cuff
Cast on 63 [71:79] sts.
Join to work in the round, being careful not to twist.

Left sock: (P1, k1tbl) 5 [7:9] times, p3, (k2, p2) 2 times, k2, (p1, k1tbl) 3 times, p2, (k1tbl, p1) 3 times, (k2, p2) 3 times, (p1, k1tbl) 7 [9:11] times.

Right sock: P2, (k1tbl, p1) 3 times, (k2, p2) 3 times, p1, (k1tbl, p1) 12 [16:20] times, (p2, k2) 3 times, (p1, k1tbl) 3 times.

Work this round 15 times more.

Leg
Left sock: (P1, k1tbl) 5 [7:9] times, p3, work chart A, p2, work chart B, p3, (k1tbl, p1) 6 [8:10] times, k1tbl.

When the 20 rounds of the charts have been completed, cont as foll:-

Next round: (P1, k1tbl) 5 [7:9] times, p3, work chart B, p2, work chart A, p3, (k1tbl, p1) 6 [8:10] times, k1tbl.

When the 20 rounds of the charts have been completed, cont as folls:-

Next round: (P1, k1tbl) 5 [7:9] times, p3, work chart A, p2, work chart B, p3, (k1tbl, p1) 6 [8:10] times, k1tbl.

When the 20 rounds of the charts have been completed, cont as folls:-

Next round: (P1, k1tbl) 5 [7:9] times, p3, work chart B, p2, work chart A, p3, (k1tbl, p1) 6 [8:10] times, k1tbl.

Cont until round 12 of the charts has been worked.

Right sock: P2, work chart B, p3, (k1tbl, p1) 12 [16:20] times, p2, work chart A.

When the 20 rounds of the charts have been completed, cont as folls:-

Next round: P2, work chart A, p3, (k1tbl, p1) 12 [16:20] times, p2, work chart B.

When the 20 rounds of the charts have been completed, cont as folls:-

Next round: P2, work chart B, p3, (k1tbl, p1) 12 [16:20] times, p2, work chart A.

When the 20 rounds of the charts have been completed, cont as folls:-

Next round: P2, work chart A, p3, (k1tbl, p1) 12 [16:20] times, p2, work chart B.

Cont until round 12 of the charts has been worked.

Heel Flap
Turn work so **WS** is facing.
Heel Flap will now be worked back and forth on the next 32[36:40] sts, beg with a **WS** row.
Keep rem 31 [35:39] sts on needles for instep.

Left sock:
Row 1 (WS): Sl1 pwise wyif, (k1, p1tbl) 6 [8:10] times, k3, (p2, k2) 2 times, p2, (k1, p1tbl) 2 times, k1, p1.
Row 2 (RS): *Sl1 pwise wyib, (p1, k1tbl) 2 times, p1, (k2, p2) 3 times, (p1, k1tbl) 6 [8:10] times, p1, k1.

Right sock:
Row 1 (WS): *Sl1 pwise wyif, (k1, p1tbl) 2 times, k1, (p2, k2) 3 times, (k1, p1tbl) 6 [8:10] times, k1, p1.
Row 2 (RS): *Sl1 pwise wyib, (p1, k1tbl) 6 [8:10] times, p3, (k2, p2) 2 times, k2, (p1, k1tbl) 2 times, p1, k1.

Work these 2 rows 15 times then work row 1 once more.

Turn Heel
Row 1 (RS): Sl1 wyib, k18 [20:22], ssk, k1, turn.
Row 2: Sl1 wyif, p7, p2tog, p1, turn.
Row 3: Sl1 wyib, k to 1 st before gap, ssk, k1, turn.
Row 4: Sl1 wyif, p to 1 st before gap, p2tog, p1, turn.
Rep rows 3 and 4 until all sts have been worked.
20 [22:24] heel sts rem.

Gusset
Set-up Round: Sl 1, k19 [21:23], pick up and knit 16 sts along edge of heel flap (1 st in each slipped st.

Left sock: (P1, k1tbl) 5 [7:9] times, p3, work chart 2 from round 13, p2.
Right sock: P2, work chart 1 from round 13, p3, (k1tbl, p1) 5 [7:9] times.

Pick up and knit 16 sts along edge of heel flap.
83 [89:95] sts.
K36 [38:40]. The start of the round is now at start of instep stitches.

Round 1: Work in pattern, (alternating charts as on leg) across instep sts, ssk, k to last 2 sts of round, k2tog.
Round 2: Work in pattern across instep sts, knit to end.
Rep these 2 rounds 9 [8:7] more times. 63 [71:79] sts.
Next round: Work in pattern, (alternating charts as on leg) across instep sts, ssk, k to end.
62 [70:78] sts rem, 31 [35:39] each on instep and sole.

Foot
Cont working evenly in patt as set until the sock measures 5cm/2in less than the desired foot length.

Toe
Round 1: Knit.
Round 2: K1, ssk, knit to 3 sts before end of instep, k2tog, k2, ssk, knit until 3 sts of round remain, k2tog, k1.

Rep these 2 rounds until 18 [22:22] sts rem.
Cut yarn, leaving a 30cm/12in tail.
Graft sts together using Kitchener stitch. Weave in ends.

CHARTS

Chart A

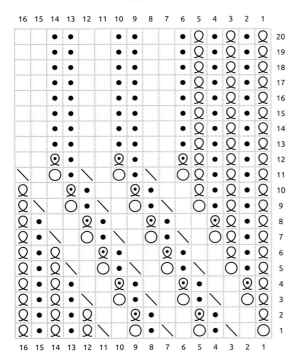

Key

☐	knit
Q	ktbl
☉	ptbl
•	purl
○	yo
/	k2tog
\	ssk

Chart B

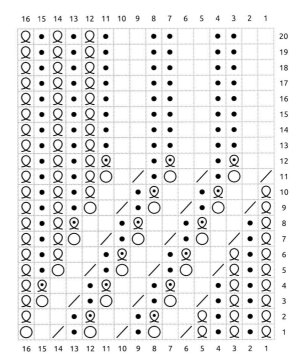

THORA

Sizes - Foot circumference

S	L	
20-23	23-25	cm
8-9	9-10	in

YARN
Rowan Fine Art
For both sizes
1 skein of shade 304 Raven

NEEDLES
2.5mm (UK 13) (US 1½) 80cm/32in circular needles or DPNs or size needed to achieve tension.
Tapestry Needle

TENSION
36 sts and 50 rows to 10cm/4in measured over st st using 2.5mm (US 1½) needles.

PATTERN NOTES
Please note there are different charts for the left and right socks.

K tbl special - For small size - k1 tbl, for large size - k2 tbl.

Cuff
Cast on 64 [72] sts.
Join to work in the round, being careful not to twist.

For Small size
Rib round: *P1, k1 tbl, rep from * to end.

For Large size
Rib round: *(P1, k 1tbl) 3 times, p1, k2tbl, rep from * to end.

For both sizes
Work this round 20 times.

Leg
Begin to work Leg chart, the chart is repeated twice across the round.
Cont to work in this way until all 48 rounds of the Leg chart have been completed.

Heel Flap
Turn work so **WS** is facing.
Heel Flap will now be worked back and forth on the next 33[38] sts, beg with a **WS** row.
Keep rem 31 [34] sts on needles for instep.

Row 1 (WS): Sl1 pwise wyif, p32 [37].
Row 2 (RS): *Sl1 pwise wyib, k1, rep from * until 1 st rem, k1.

Work these 2 rows 15 times then work row 1 once more.

Turn Heel
Row 1 (RS): Sl1 wyib, k17 [20], ssk, k1, turn.
Row 2: Sl1 wyif, p4 [5], p2tog, p1, turn.
Row 3: Sl1 wyib, k to 1 st before gap, ssk, k1, turn.
Row 4: Sl1 wyif, p to 1 st before gap, p2tog, p1, turn.
Rep rows 3 and 4 until all sts have been worked.
19 [22] heel sts rem.

Gusset
Set-up Round: Sl 1, k18 [21], pick up and knit 16 sts along edge of heel flap (1 st in each
slipped st; work instep chart, pick up and knit 16 sts along edge of heel flap.82 [88] sts.
K35 [38]. The start of the round is now at start of instep stitches.

Round 1: Work in pattern as set on instep chart across instep sts, ssk, k to last 2 sts of round, k2tog.
Round 2: Work in pattern as set on instep chart across instep sts, knit to end.
Rep these 2 rounds 8 more times. 64 [70] sts rem, 31 [34] on instep and 33[36] on sole.

Foot

Cont working evenly in patt as set until instep chart is complete, then rep round 48 until sock measures 5cm/2in less than the desired foot length.

Toe

Toe Set-up: K32[35], ssk, knit until 3 sts rem, k2tog, k1. 62 [68] sts rem, 31 [34] on instep and sole.

Round 1: Knit.
Round 2: K1, ssk, knit to 3 sts before end of instep, k2tog, k2, ssk, knit until 3 sts rem, k2tog, k1.

Rep these 2 rounds until 18 [24] sts rem.
Cut yarn, leaving a 30cm/12in tail. Graft sts together using Kitchener stitch. Weave in ends.

CHARTS

Instep Left

Instep Right

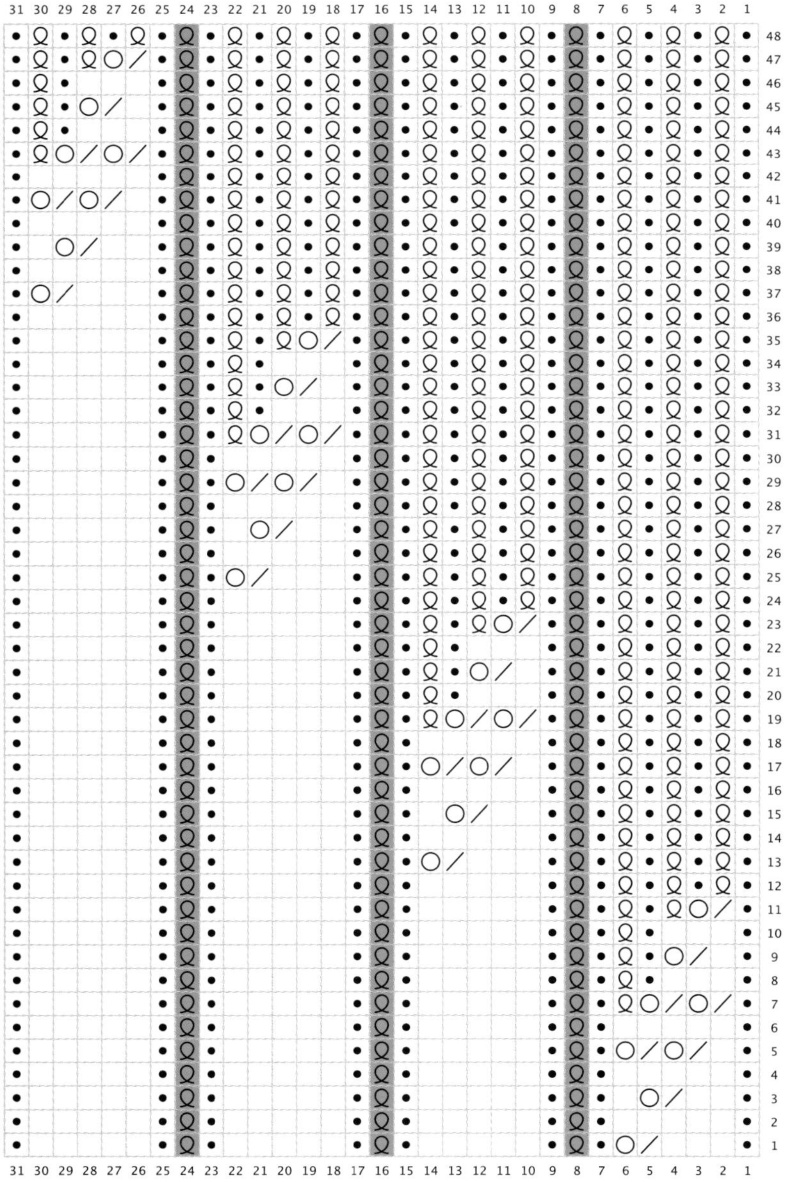

Key

- knit
- • purl
- ktbl
- yo
- ssk
- k2tog
- k tbl special

Leg Left

32 31 30 29 28 27 26 25 24 23 22 21 20 19 18 17 16 15 14 13 12 11 10 9 8 7 6 5 4 3 2 1

32 31 30 29 28 27 26 25 24 23 22 21 20 19 18 17 16 15 14 13 12 11 10 9 8 7 6 5 4 3 2 1

Leg Right

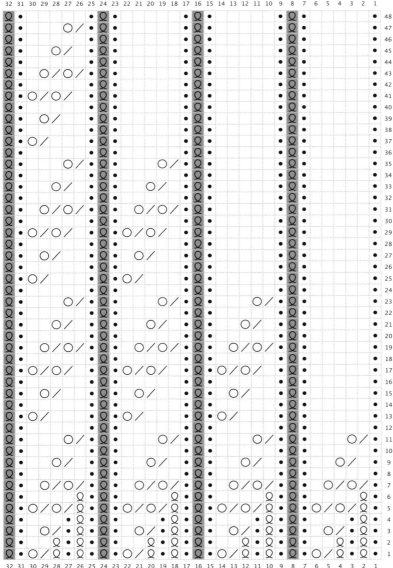

Key

☐	knit
•	purl
Ω	ktbl
○	yo
＼	ssk
／	k2tog
Ω	k tbl special

ELLERY

Sizes - Foot circumference

S	M	L	
20	23	25	cm
8	9	10	in

YARN
Rowan Fine Art
For all sizes
1 skein of shade 306 Lapwing

NEEDLES
2.5mm (UK 13) (US 1½) 80cm/32in circular needles or DPNs or size needed to achieve tension. Cable Needle Tapestry Needle

TENSION
36 sts and 50 rows to 10cm/4in measured over st st using 2.5mm (US 1½) needles.

1/1 RT: Slip next st to cable needle and place at back of work, k1 tbl, then k1 tbl from cable needle.
1/1 LT: Slip next st to cable needle and place at front of work, k1 tbl, then k1 tbl from cable needle.
1/1 RPT: Slip next st to cable needle and place at back of work, k1 tbl, then p1 from cable needle.
1/1 LPT: Slip next st to cable needle and place at front of work, p1, then k1 tbl from cable needle.

Cuff
Cast on 64 [72:80] sts.
Join to work in the round, being careful not to twist.
Rib round: (K2[4,6], work rib chart, k2[4,6]) twice.

Work the rib round 16 times.

Leg
Next round: (K2[4,6], work Chart A, k2[4,6]) twice.
Work in this way until Chart A has been completed 3 more times (30 rounds).
Next round: (K2[4,6], work Chart B, k4[8,12], work Chart A, k2[4,6].
Work in this way until Chart A has been completed 3 more times and round 1 has been worked once more (31 rounds).

Heel Flap
Turn work so **WS** is facing.
Heel Flap will now be worked back and forth on the next 32[36:40] sts, beg with a **WS** row.
Keep rem 32[36:40] sts on needles for instep.

Row 1 (WS): Sl1 pwise wyif, p1[3:5], k3, (p2tbl, k2, p1tbl, k2, p1tbl, k2) twice, p2tbl, k3, p2[4:6].
Row 2 (RS): *Sl1 pwise wyib, k1[3:5], p3, (k2tbl, p2, k1tbl, p2, k1tbl, p2) twice, k2tbl, p3, k2[4:6].

Work these 2 rows 15 times then work row 1 once more.

Turn Heel
Row 1 (RS): Sl1 wyib, k18 [20:22], ssk, k1, turn.
Row 2: Sl1 wyif, p7, p2tog, p1, turn.
Row 3: Sl1 wyib, k to 1 st before gap, ssk, k1, turn.
Row 4: Sl1 wyif, p to 1 st before gap, p2tog, p1, turn.
Rep rows 3 and 4 until all sts have been worked.
20 [22:24] heel sts rem.

Gusset
Set-up Round: Sl 1, k19 [21:23], pick up and knit 16 sts along edge of heel flap (1 st in each slipped st, k2[4:6], work round 32 of Chart B, k2[4:6], pick up and knit 16 sts along edge of heel flap.
84 [90:96] sts.
K36 [38:40]. The start of the round is now at start of instep stitches.

Round 1: K2 [4:6], cont to work Chart B, k2 [4:6], ssk, k to last 2 sts of round, k2tog.
Round 2: Work in pattern across instep sts, knit to end.

Once rounds 33-48 of Chart B have been completed; k2[4:6], work Chart A, k2[4:6].

Rep these 2 rounds 9 [8:7] more times. 64 [72:80] sts rem, 32 [36:40] each on instep and sole.

Foot
Cont working evenly in patt as set until Chart A has been completed 3 times.

Next round: K2[4:6] work rib chart, k2[4:6], knit to end.
Cont working evenly in pattern as set until the sock measures 5cm/2in less than the desired foot length.

Toe
Round 1: Knit.
Round 2: K1[3:5], ssk, knit to 3[5:7] sts before end of instep, k2tog, k2[6:10], ssk, knit until 3[5:7] sts remain, k2tog, k1[3:5].

Rep these 2 rounds until 20 [24:24] sts rem.
Cut yarn, leaving a 30cm/12in tail. Graft sts together using Kitchener stitch. Weave in ends.

CHARTS

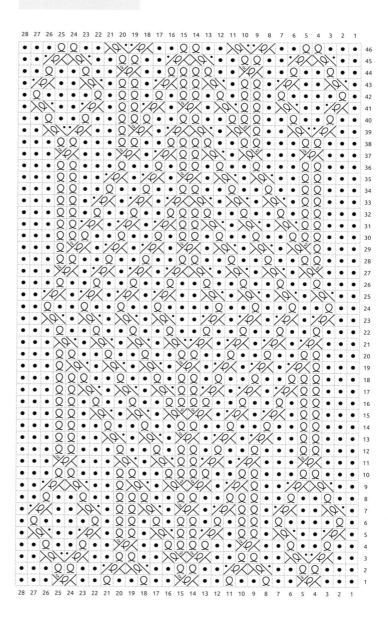

Chart A

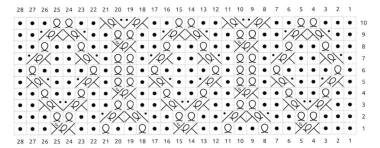

| 28 | 27 | 26 | 25 | 24 | 23 | 22 | 21 | 20 | 19 | 18 | 17 | 16 | 15 | 14 | 13 | 12 | 11 | 10 | 9 | 8 | 7 | 6 | 5 | 4 | 3 | 2 | 1 | |

Rib

| 28 | 27 | 26 | 25 | 24 | 23 | 22 | 21 | 20 | 19 | 18 | 17 | 16 | 15 | 14 | 13 | 12 | 11 | 10 | 9 | 8 | 7 | 6 | 5 | 4 | 3 | 2 | 1 | |

| 28 | 27 | 26 | 25 | 24 | 23 | 22 | 21 | 20 | 19 | 18 | 17 | 16 | 15 | 14 | 13 | 12 | 11 | 10 | 9 | 8 | 7 | 6 | 5 | 4 | 3 | 2 | 1 | |

Key

☐ knit

● purl

 Q ktbl

✗ 1/1 RT

✗ 1/1 LT

✗ 1/1 RPT

✗ 1/1 LPT

HELPFUL TECHNIQUES

KITCHENER STITCH (GRAFTING)

Every sock in this book uses kitchener stitch to close the toe stitches. This tutorial shows you how, and gives tips on making the graft stitches neat and tidy.

1. Holding needles parallel to each other, thread a tapestry needle with the yarn tail. Insert the needle into the first stitch on the needle closest to you as if to purl and pull it through, leaving the stitch on the needle.

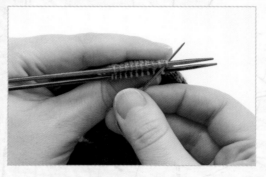

2. Insert the needle into the first stitch on the needle furthest from you as if to knit and pull it through, leaving the stitch on the needle.

3. Insert the needle into the first stitch on the needle closest to you as if to knit and pull it through, slipping the stitch off the needle

4. Insert the needle into the first stitch on the needle closest to you as if to purl and pull it through, leaving the stitch on the needle.

5. Insert the needle into the first stitch on the needle furthest from you as if to purl and pull it through, slipping the stitch off the needle

6. Insert the needle into the first stitch on the needle furthest from you as if to knit and pull it through, leaving the stitch on the needle.

Repeat steps 3-6 until all the live stitches have been grafted together. The grafted stitches will be looser than the knitted stitches around them. Use the tapestry needle to neaten them: starting at the first stitch to be grafted, pull each stitch until it matches the knitted stitches on the toe. Take the yarn to the inside of the sock and weave in the end to finish.

LONG-TAIL CAST-ON

This cast-on method gives a firm but flexible edge that is perfect for socks

1. Measure approximately 1m [1yd] of yarn, place the yarn over the needle with the ball at the rear and the tail of the yarn towards you. Use your forefinger to hold the yarn on the needle.

2. Using the tail end of the yarn, make a loop of yarn around your thumb as shown.

3. Put the needle tip into the loop.

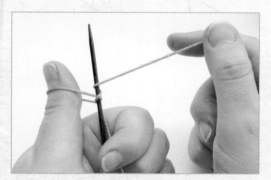

4. Use your right hand to wrap the yarn from the ball side around the needle tip.

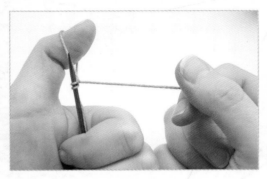

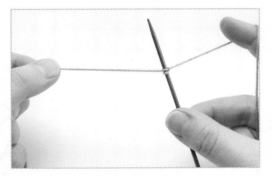

5. Use your thumb to lift the loop off the end of the needle, thus making the first (formed by holding the yarn over the needle) and second stitches.

6. Gently tighten both ends of the yarn (tail and ball sides).

7. Continue as set: repeat steps 2 to 6 until you have cast on the desired number of stitches.

ABBREVIATIONS

Cdd: Centered double decrease: slip 2 sts as if to k2tog, k1, pass the 2 slipped sts over

Increase 1 to 3: Knit, purl, knit in to the next stitch, 2 stitches increased

K: Knit

K2tog: Knit two stitches together as one stitch

Kwise: Knitwise, as if to knit

P: Purl

Pwise: Purlwise, as if to purl

P2tog: Purl two stitches together as one stitch

Rem: Remaining

Rep: Repeat

RS: Right side of work

Sl: Slip the next stitch from left to right purl-wise.

Ssk: Slip one stitch as if to knit, slip the next stitch as if to knit, insert left needle into front of these two stitches and knit them together.

St: stitch

Tbl: through the back loop

Wrap 3: K1tbl, p1, k1tbl onto cable needle, wrap yarn twice around these stitches by bringing yarn to front of work between the left needle and the cable needle and wrapping yarn to back of work between cable needle and right needle, then slip the 3 stitches from the cable needle to the right needle.

WS: Wrong side of work

Wyib: with yarn in back

Wyif: with yarn in front

Yo: Yarn over

1/1 RC: Slip next st to cable needle and place at back of work, k1, then k1 from cable needle.

1/1 LC: Slip next st to cable needle and place at front of work, k1, then k1 from cable needle.

1/1 RT: Slip next st to cable needle and place at back of work, k1 tbl, then k1 tbl from cable needle

1/1 LT: Slip next st to cable needle and place at front of work, k1 tbl, then k1 tbl from cable needle

1/1 LPC: Slip next st to cable needle and place at front of work, p1, then k1 from cable needle

1/1 RPC: Slip next st to cable needle and place at back of work, k1, then p1 from cable needle

1/1 RPT: Slip next st to cable needle and place at back of work, k1 tbl, then p1 from cable needle

1/1 LPT: Slip next st to cable needle and place at front of work, p1, then k1 tbl from cable needle

2/1 LT: Slip next 2 sts to cable needle and place at front of work, k1, then k2 from cable needle

2/1 RT: Slip next st to cable needle and place at back of work, k2, then k1 from cable needle

2/1 RPC: Slip next st to cable needle and place at back of work, k2, then p1 from cable needle.

2/1 LPC: Slip next 2 sts to cable needle and place at front of work, p1, then k2 from cable needle.

2/1 LPT: Slip next 2 sts to cable needle and place at front of work, p1, then knit 2 stitches tbl from cable needle

2/1 RPT: Slip next st to cable needle and place at back of work, knit 2 stitches tbl, then p1 from cable needle

2/2 RC: Slip next 2 sts to cable needle and place at back of work, k2, then k2 from cable needle.

2/2 LC: Slip next 2 sts to cable needle and place at front of work, k2, then k2 from cable needle.

STOCKISTS

AUSTRALIA: Australian Country Spinners, Pty Ltd, Level 7, 409 St. Kilda Road, Melbourne Vic 3004.
Tel: 03 9380 3888 Fax: 03 9820 0989
Email: customerservice@auspinners.com.au

AUSTRIA: Coats Harlander Ges GmbH, Autokaderstraße 29, 1210 Wien, Österreich Tel: 00800 26 27 28 00
Fax: (00) 49 7644 802-133 Email: coats.harlander@coats.com
Web: www.coatscrafts.at

BELGIUM: Coats N.V., c/o Coats GmbH Kaiserstr.1 79341 Kenzingen Germany
Tel: 0032 (0) 800 77 89 2 Fax: 00 49 7644 802 133
Email: sales.coatsninove@coats.com Web: www.coatscrafts.be

BULGARIA: Coats Bulgaria, 7 Magnaurska Shkola Str., BG-1784 Sofia, Bulgaria
Tel: (+359 2) 976 77 41 Fax: (+359 2) 976 77 20 Email: officebg@coats.com
Web: www.coatsbulgaria.bg

CANADA: Westminster Fibers, 10 Roybridge Gate, Suite 200, Vaughan, Ontario
L4H 3M8 Tel: (800) 263-2354 Fax: 905-856-5585 Email: info@westminsterfibers.com

CHINA: Coats Shanghai Ltd, No 9 Building , Baosheng Road, Songjiang Industrial Zone, Shanghai. Tel: (86- 21) 13816681825
Fax: (86-21) 57743733-326 Email: victor.li@coats.com

CYPRUS: Coats Bulgaria, 7 Magnaurska Shkola Str., BG-1784 Sofia, Bulgaria
Tel: (+359 2) 976 77 41 Fax: (+359 2) 976 77 20
Email: officebg@coats.com Web: www.coatscrafts.com.cy

CZECH REPUBLIC: Coats Czecho s.r.o.Staré Město 246 569 32
Tel: (420) 461616633 Email: galanterie@coats.com

ESTONIA: Coats Eesti AS, Ampri tee 9/4, 74001 Viimsi Harjumaa
Tel: +372 630 6250 Fax: +372 630 6260 Email: info@coats.ee
Web: www.coatscrafts.co.ee

DENMARK: Coats Expotex AB, Stationsvägen 2, 516 21 Dalsjöfors
Tel: (45) 35 86 90 49 E-mail: info.dk@coats.com

FINLAND: Coats Opti Crafts Oy, Huhtimontie 6 04200 KERAVA
Tel: (358) 9 274871 Fax: (358) 9 2426 186
Email: coatsopti.sales@coats.com www.coatscrafts.fi

FRANCE: Coats France, c/o Coats GmbH, Kaiserstr.1, 79341 Kenzingen, Germany
Tel: (0) 0810 06 00 02 Email: artsdufil@coats.com Web: www.coatscrafts.fr

GERMANY: Coats GmbH, Kaiserstr, 1, 79341 Kenzingen, Germany
Tel: 0049 7644 802 222 Email: kenzingen.vertrieb@coats.com
Fax: 0049 7644 802 300 Web: www.coatsgmbh.de

GREECE: Coats Bulgaria, 7 Magnaurska Shkola Str., BG-1784 Sofia, Bulgaria
Tel: (+359 2) 976 77 41 Fax: (+359 2) 976 77 20
Email: officebg@coats.com Web: www.coatscrafts.gr

HOLLAND: Coats B.V., c/o Coats GmbH Kaiserstr.1 79341 Kenzingen, Germany
Tel: 0031 (0) 800 02 26 6488 Fax: 00 49 7644 802 133
Email: sales.coatsninove@coats.com Web: www.coatscrafts.be

HONG KONG: East Unity Company Ltd, Unit B2, 7/F., Block B, Kailey Industrial Centre, 12 Fung Yip Street, Chai Wan Tel: (852)2869 7110
Email: eastunityco@yahoo.com.hk

ICELAND: Storkurinn, Laugavegi 59, 101 Reykjavik
Tel: (354) 551 8258 Email: storkurinn@simnet.is

ITALY: Coats Cucirini srl, Viale Sarca no 223, 20126 Milano
Tel: 02636151 Fax: 0266111701

KOREA: Coats Korea Co. Ltd, 5F Eyeon B/D, 935-40 Bangbae-Dong, 137-060
Tel: (82) 2 521 6262 Fax: (82) 2 521 5181 Email: rozenpark@coats.com

LATVIA: Coats Latvija SIA, Mukusalas str. 41 b, Riga LV-1004
Tel: +371 67 625173 Fax: +371 67 892758
Email: info.latvia@coats.com Web: www.coatscrafts.lv

LEBANON: y.knot, Saifi Village, Mkhalissiya Street 162, Beirut
Tel: (961) 1 992211 Fax: (961) 1 315553 Email: y.knot@cyberia.net.lb

LITHUANIA & RUSSIA: Coats Lietuva UAB, A. Juozapaviciaus str. 6/2,
LT-09310 Vilnius Tel: +370 527 30971 Fax: +370 527 2305 Email: info@coats.lt
Web: www.coatscrafts.lt

LUXEMBOURG: Coats N.V., c/o Coats GmbH Kaiserstr.1 79341 Kenzingen,
Germany Tel: 00 49 7644 802 222 Fax: 00 49 7644 802 133 Email: sales.
coatsninove@coats.com Web: www.coatscrafts.be

MALTA: John Gregory Ltd, 8 Ta'Xbiex Sea Front, Msida MSD 1512, Malta
Tel: +356 2133 0202 Fax: +356 2134 4745 Email: raygreg@onvol.net

MEXICO: Estambres Crochet SA de CV, PO Box SANTAMARIA,
64650 MONTERREY

NEW ZEALAND: ACS New Zealand, 1 March Place, Belfast, Christchurch Tel: 64 3 323 6665 Fax: 64 3 323 6660

NORWAY: Coats Knappehuset AS, Pb 100 Ulset, 5873 Bergen
Tel: (47) 55 53 93 00 Fax: (47) 55 53 93 93 E-mail: kundeservice@coats.com

PORTUGAL: Companhia de Linha Coats & Clark, Quinta de Cravel,
4400 Vilanova de Gaia Portugal Tel: 00 351 223 770700

SINGAPORE: Golden Dragon Store, 101 Upper Cross Street #02-51,
People's Park Centre, Singapore 058357 Tel: (65) 6 5358454 Fax: (65) 6 2216278
Email: gdscraft@hotmail.com

SLOVAKIA: Coats s.r.o.Kopčianska 94851 01 Bratislava
Tel: (421) 263532314 Email: galanteria@coats.com

SOUTH AFRICA: Arthur Bales LTD, 62 4th Avenue, Linden 2195
Tel: (27) 11 888 2401 Fax: (27) 11 782 6137 Email: arthurb@new.co.za

SPAIN: Coats Fabra, Sant Adria 20, 08030 Barcelona
Tel: (34) 932908400 Fax: 932908409 Email: atencion.clientes@coats.com

SWEDEN: Coats Expotex AB, Stationsvägen 2, 516 21 Dalsjöfors
Tel: (46) 33 720 79 00 Fax: 46 31 47 16 50 E-mail: kundtjanst@coats.com

SWITZERLAND: Coats Stroppel AG, Stroppelstrasse 20, 5417 Untersiggenthal,
Schweiz Tel: 00800 2627 2800 Fax: 0049 7644 802 133
Email: coats.stroppel@coats.com Web: www.coatscrafts.ch

TAIWAN: Cactus Quality Co Ltd, 7FL-2, No. 140, Sec.2 Roosevelt Rd, Taipei,
10084 Taiwan, R.O.C. Tel: 00886-2-23656527 Fax: 886-2-23656503
Email: cqcl@ms17.hinet.net

THAILAND: Global Wide Trading, 10 Lad Prao Soi 88, Bangkok 10310
Tel: 00 662 933 9019 Fax: 00 662 933 9110 Email: global.wide@yahoo.com

U.S.A.: Westminster Fibers, 8 Shelter Drive, Greer, South Carolina, 29650
Tel: (800) 445-9276 Fax: 864-879-9432 Email: info@westminsterfibers.com

U.K: Rowan, Green Lane Mill, Holmfirth, West Yorkshire, England HD9 2DX
Tel: +44 (0) 1484 681881 Fax: +44 (0) 1484 687920 Email: ccuk.sales@coats.com
Web: www.knitrowan.com

For stockists in all other countries please contact Rowan for details

AUTHORS ACKNOWLEDGEMENTS

Thanks to my husband for his unwavering support and offers of help with the 'straight knitting'. Thanks to Emma and Louise for the sock knitting skills and thanks to Sarah, for many things, not least of which is showing me the Aurora Borealis.

PUBLISHERS ACKNOWLEDGEMENTS

The publisher would like to thank Sarah Hatton for her help and support in the production of this title and checking patterns. Sam Sloan for his clean, detailed photography and welcoming the whole team into his home for the photoshoot.

Jenna Louise Hollins for being an excellent foot model, and bringing to life the sock designs.

Q
QUAIL